KT-382-600

# TopGear

BEST BITS

# The Races v.2

*BBC Children's Books*
*Published by the Penguin Group*
*Penguin Books Ltd, 80 Strand, London WC2R 0RL, England*
*Penguin Group (Australia) Ltd, 250 Camberwell Road, Camberwell, Victoria 3124, Australia (a division of Pearson Australia Group Pty Ltd)*
*Canada, India, New Zealand, South Africa*

*Published by BBC Children's Books, 2009*

*This edition produced for The Book People Ltd, Hall Wood Avenue, Haydock, St Helens, WA11 9UL*

*10 9 8 7 6 5 4 3 2 1*

*Written by Jonathan Empson*



*ISBN: 978-1-40590-656-2*

*Printed in China*

# Contents

*on water!

# Introduction

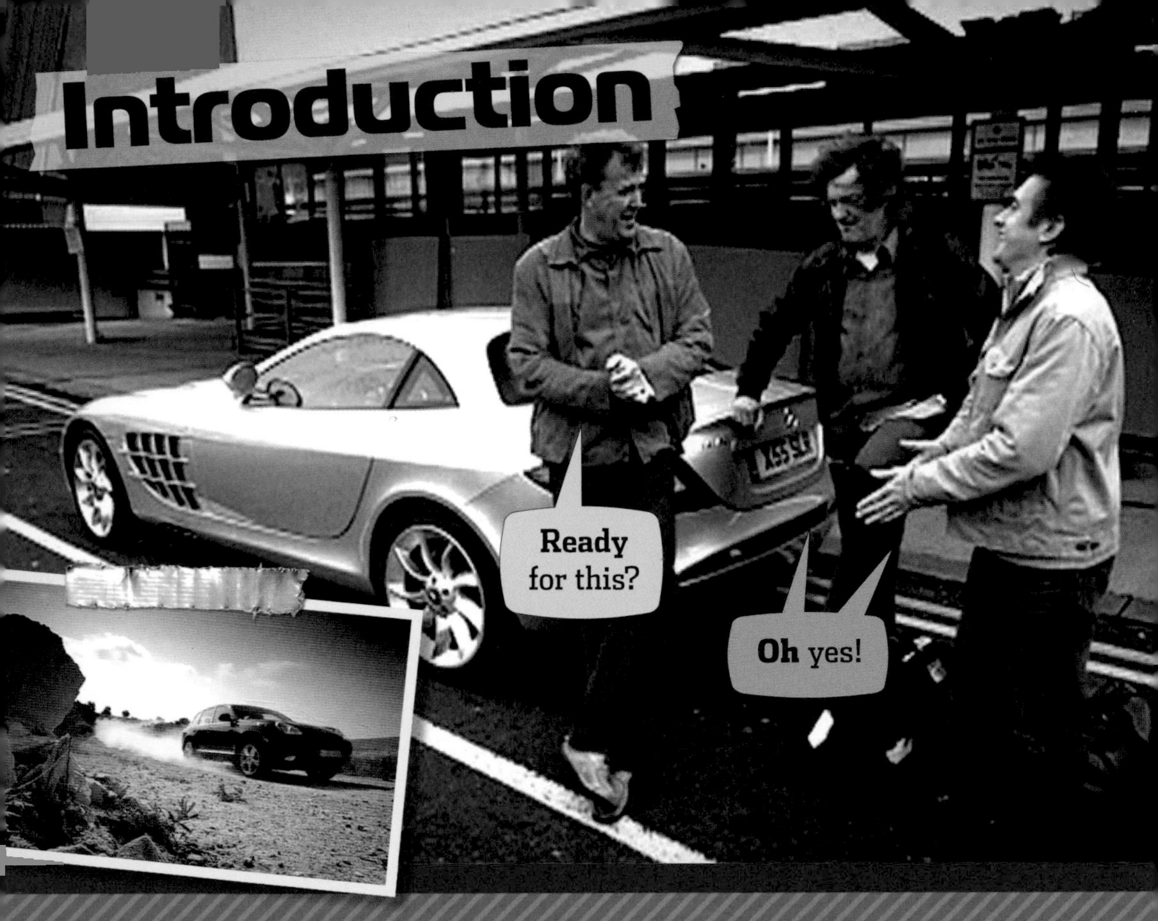


Welcome to Volume II of The Races, where Top Gear aims once again to prove the superiority of cars by racing them against other, more boring forms of transport. In Volume I, the cars lost a few of the contests, which was very embarrassing.

So this time, Top Gear are making it easier on themselves by taking on really slow things like cyclists and walkers and ferries. How can they lose? They're so confident they'll score six out of six victories, Captain Slow himself, James May, is allowed behind the wheel.

These are all genuine, real-world tests with very sensible aims. For instance, is a car faster across London than public transport? Is it faster across Budapest than a bicycle?

**If you find yourself on holiday in Cyprus, is it better to get around in a Porsche Cayenne, or by throwing yourself out of a helicopter with a parachute strapped to your back?**

**For the many Norwegian Top Gear fans who are scared of flying, we also answer the vital question: What's the best way to get from London to Oslo in a hurry?**

**Discover the answers to these and other important questions in the following pages.**

## Let the races begin!

# Race Across London

**This race is a matter of pride for the car. It's up against a bike, boat and public transport. This one should be in the bag. Although James *is* behind the wheel...**

The North Circular is London's original ring road. It can take you all the way from Kew in the west to City Airport in the east... eventually. It's one of the busiest roads in this traffic-clogged capital. So what is the best way to handle the commute...and survive? Our team decided to find out: three men and a Stig, four modes of transport. Who'd win a race to the City Airport check-in desk?

## The Competitors

### Bicycle: Richard Hammond

Richard once more has an excuse to squeeze into tight-fitting clothing as he prepares to pedal across the city. He'll be trying to avoid taxis, buses and choking on exhaust fumes on his lightweight, carbon-fibre Specialized Series Limited. At least London's slow traffic makes cycling a bit less dangerous. Compared to, say, firing yourself across the city using a giant catapult.

It **is** quite expensive.

### Car: James May

It's up to James to uphold the honour of the car in this race. He'll be piloting a quiet and powerful 5.5-litre Mercedes GL: 17ft long and "the Chelsea-ist of all the Chelsea tractors". James lives in London, so surely he can't get lost. And even Captain Slow must be able to keep up with London's sluggish traffic.

It's about 6.5 feet wide... it weighs **2.5 tons!**

## Public Transport: The Stig

The Stig must enter a strange world where vehicles are driven by other people… and at less than maximum speed. These vehicles are called 'buses' and 'trains'. Some of them travel on rails, underground! It's all very unnatural. Some people might say it's cruel to put the Stig through this. No-one knows quite how he will handle it. There could be a bloodbath.

## Boat: Jeremy Clarkson

The River Thames twists a lot, but it does run via Kew Bridge straight past City Airport. Jeremy will take a break from terrorising other road users and take to the water – where he can terrorise ducks instead. Naturally he won't be rowing – or even driving a pickup with a huge outboard motor bolted to the tailgate. No, he'll be in a £52,000 Cougar sport racing boat powered by a 225hp, 3.5-litre Honda engine.

## And They're Off!

It's 8.32 on a Monday morning: peak rush-hour time. It's humid. Sweaty, even. Not good for cycling, or travelling by Tube while wearing a racing suit and full-face helmet. Jeremy does the countdown: "3... 2..." But the Stig jumps the start!

Hold on, he's **jumped** the gun!

*Richard is fastest away. James is also confident.*

This **is** a car. This **is** a car **programme.** I shall **not** let you down.

Jeremy is even more confident in his 75mph powerboat. The only problem: there's a 9mph speed limit on this part of the river – and the river's meanders will make his journey 7 miles longer.

A 'big red car' stops in front of the Stig, so he gets on it. As he has no concept of money, he pays his bus fare using something called an 'Oyster card'.

Richard zooms along the bus lanes – which cyclists are allowed to use. Trouble is, so are buses.
James is slowed by rush-hour traffic. He calls Richard to check his progress, but all he gets is static.
Chabkkmmnn zamtsskkrrkkk
Do you want a lift?
With nothing better to do, Captain Clarkson decides to call Captain Slow, who's reached Hammersmith Broadway (he thinks). James reports on his last call to Richard.
BBLLBBLBBLLBLBLBLBLBLLBBRR
It sounded like his **face** was rubbing along the **road**. He may have **had it** already.
Keep: right.
I **knew** that!

With 25 minutes gone, Richard is leading, James is 2nd, the Stig is 3rd and Jeremy is last. But Richard is getting stressed out by the big red cars. So is James.

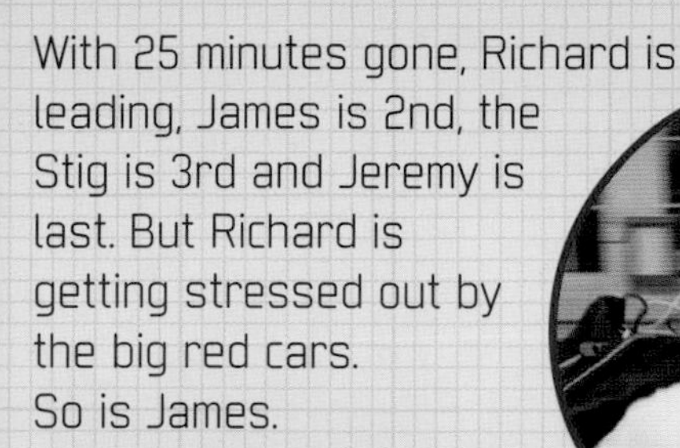

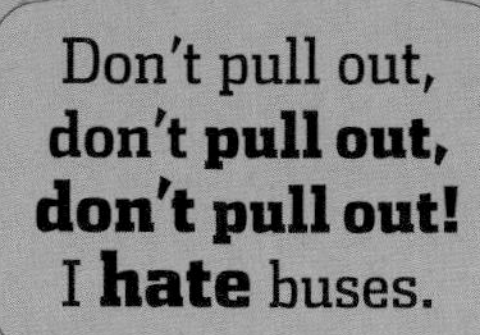

The Stig tries an 'underground car'.

Richard is now getting stressed out by traffic lights.

Not **another** set of &*%$£ lights!

35 minutes in, the positions are the same, but car is closing on cyclist near the Royal Albert Hall.

I'll give you a friendly **peep** as I go past.

Oh **crikey**, it's the rozzers.

Then the police stop James to check his camera crew's permit, delaying him by four minutes.

Richard is trying to keep up a speed of 19mph. He's on the Embankment, which runs alongside the river – so where's Jeremy? He's a minute from Wandsworth Bridge – and from then on, "there's no speed limit at all".

Richard is 8 miles from the airport, Jeremy 17 miles – but now going much faster. The Stig is on the Docklands Light Railway, the last leg. James is also closing in as he clears central London traffic, but he's rarely going faster than 25mph.

Jeremy passes the police at 45mph, legally. But he runs into a bit of congestion too – tourist boats.

Then Jeremy clears Tower Bridge and accelerates to 50mph.

James is now last, the Stig in third, but as Jeremy tops 70mph, has he overtaken Richard?

Jeremy scythes through the Thames Barrier. Richard sees the signs for the City Airport.

To get to the check-in desk, Jeremy has to tie up his boat and leg it for the last stretch.

## The Winner

Jeremy arrives at the check-in desk... to find Richard has beaten him to it. And he's not even out of breath.

The Stig take third place... and James, 15 minutes behind, is dead last.

You've **ruined** Top Gear.

OK, **between** us we've ruined Top Gear.

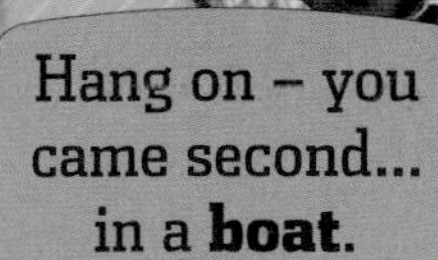

# Porsche Cayenne vs Red Devil

**Is a Porsche faster than a man dropping out of the sky? Richard Hammond decided there was only one place where he could find out: Cyprus. (Actually, he could have done this race anywhere, but he likes the weather in Cyprus.)**

## The Race

Richard will drive a Porsche Cayenne down a 2.5-mile stretch of bumpy gravel road full of blind bends. It's normally used for the Cyprus Rally – so it's a bit rougher than the M1 or the roads around Harrods, where Cayennes normally hang out.

As Richard leaves the starting line, a man will throw himself out of a helicopter 10,000ft (that's 2 miles) overhead and try and skydive to the finish line first – i.e. travelling 2.5 miles horizontally while all the time plummeting to earth.

The skydiver should be able to average 60mph sideways. But can the Cayenne match him?

## The Competitors

### Porsche Cayenne Turbo S

This is the most powerful production car that Porsche makes. Its 4.8-litre V8 pumps out 550bhp. It has to be powerful, to get its 2.5 tonnes to 60mph inside 5.2 seconds. It costs £90,000 – and a lot more than that if you actually want to drive it anywhere (such as home from the dealer), because it's a thirsty beast. The Cayenne has four-wheel drive, with clever Porsche traction management and active air suspension. But how will it cope with a road this rough, carrying a big, beefy man like Richard Hammond?

It's physics gone mad!

### Red Devil

Lance Corporal Mac McAuliffe is a member of the Parachute Regiment's Red Devils, who do amazing aerial stunts – without planes. He'll use a special 'flying squirrel' Phoenix-Fly Vampire 2 wingsuit to help him fly sideways faster than he's falling vertically. Without it, he'd be splattered over the landscape long before he reached the finish line.

He will have to open his parachute to slow down at some point – and he can't leave it too late.

## And They're Off!

Richard waits at the start line. Mac stands by the door of the helicopter, hovering directly overhead – it's using a GPS for accurate positioning.

Mac jumps out of the plane. Richard almost crashes straightaway.

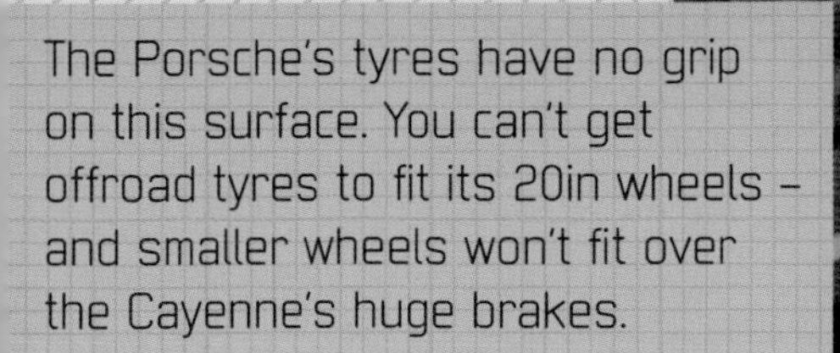

The Porsche's tyres have no grip on this surface. You can't get offroad tyres to fit its 20in wheels – and smaller wheels won't fit over the Cayenne's huge brakes.

Mac is now travelling at 100mph horizontally, 30mph vertically.

Richard spots Mac overhead.

At the halfway point, the Red Devil is well ahead. But soon he'll have to open his chute and slow down.

The Cayenne hits another big dip.

At 2500ft, Mac opens his chute.
Richard gets out of the hills and onto the flat.
Mac spirals down, lines up for the finish line.
SSSKKRRREEEEEEEE
Just give me a **little** bit more **now!**

## The Winner

Mac crosses the line first – barely 30 metres in front of Richard. (And to make matters worse, as the defeated Richard drove away in the Porsche afterwards, he crashed it into the car of one of the production crew – hard enough to set off the airbags.)

# McLaren Mercedes SLR VS Boat

**By car, the Norwegian city of Oslo is a 1320-mile drive from London's Heathrow airport. You have to go via France. And Belgium. And the Netherlands, Germany, Denmark and Sweden. Surely it's faster to get there straight across the North Sea (by ship, obviously)?**

Jeremy (in the car of course) decided to race James and Richard (the sailors) to find out. As no ships sail from Heathrow, the Hamster and Captain Slow will first have to fly to Newcastle to catch one.

What is the **fastest** way of getting from London ... to Oslo?

X55 SLR

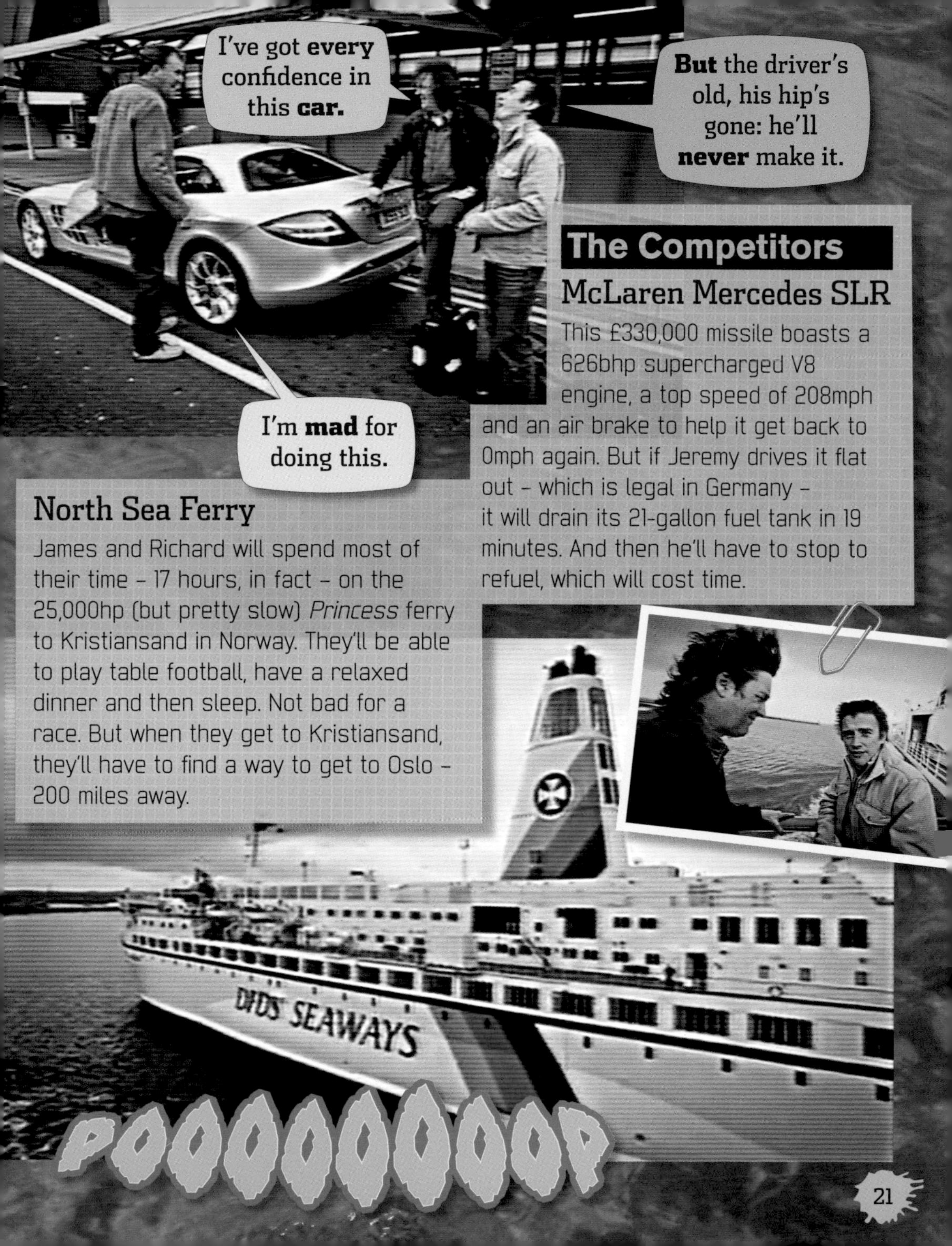


## The Competitors

### McLaren Mercedes SLR

This £330,000 missile boasts a 626bhp supercharged V8 engine, a top speed of 208mph and an air brake to help it get back to 0mph again. But if Jeremy drives it flat out – which is legal in Germany – it will drain its 21-gallon fuel tank in 19 minutes. And then he'll have to stop to refuel, which will cost time.

### North Sea Ferry

James and Richard will spend most of their time – 17 hours, in fact – on the 25,000hp (but pretty slow) *Princess* ferry to Kristiansand in Norway. They'll be able to play table football, have a relaxed dinner and then sleep. Not bad for a race. But when they get to Kristiansand, they'll have to find a way to get to Oslo – 200 miles away.

## And They're Off!

Richard and James head for the check-in desk, even breaking into a light jog in their eagerness to beat Jeremy – who screams away from the kerb, heading to Kent and the Channel Tunnel.

Richard and James check in... and wait an hour for their flight to board. Jeremy sets his satnav for Oslo... but gets stuck behind a dawdling driver.

*The Channel Tunnel is straight ahead. Though not according to the satnav.*

Turn: left

It's straight ahead! I can **read**, you useless harridan!

*James and Richard finally take off.*

A **part** of me **really** wants that car to win – but **all** of me wants Jeremy to **lose.**

That's **enough** health and safety: can we **go** now?

Jeremy finds the 1.30pm Channel Tunnel train he was planning to catch doesn't exist. He waits.

James and Richard arrive in Newcastle and get a bus to the port. Jeremy finally gets his car on the train, but is further delayed by endless safety announcements – in two languages.

X55 SLR

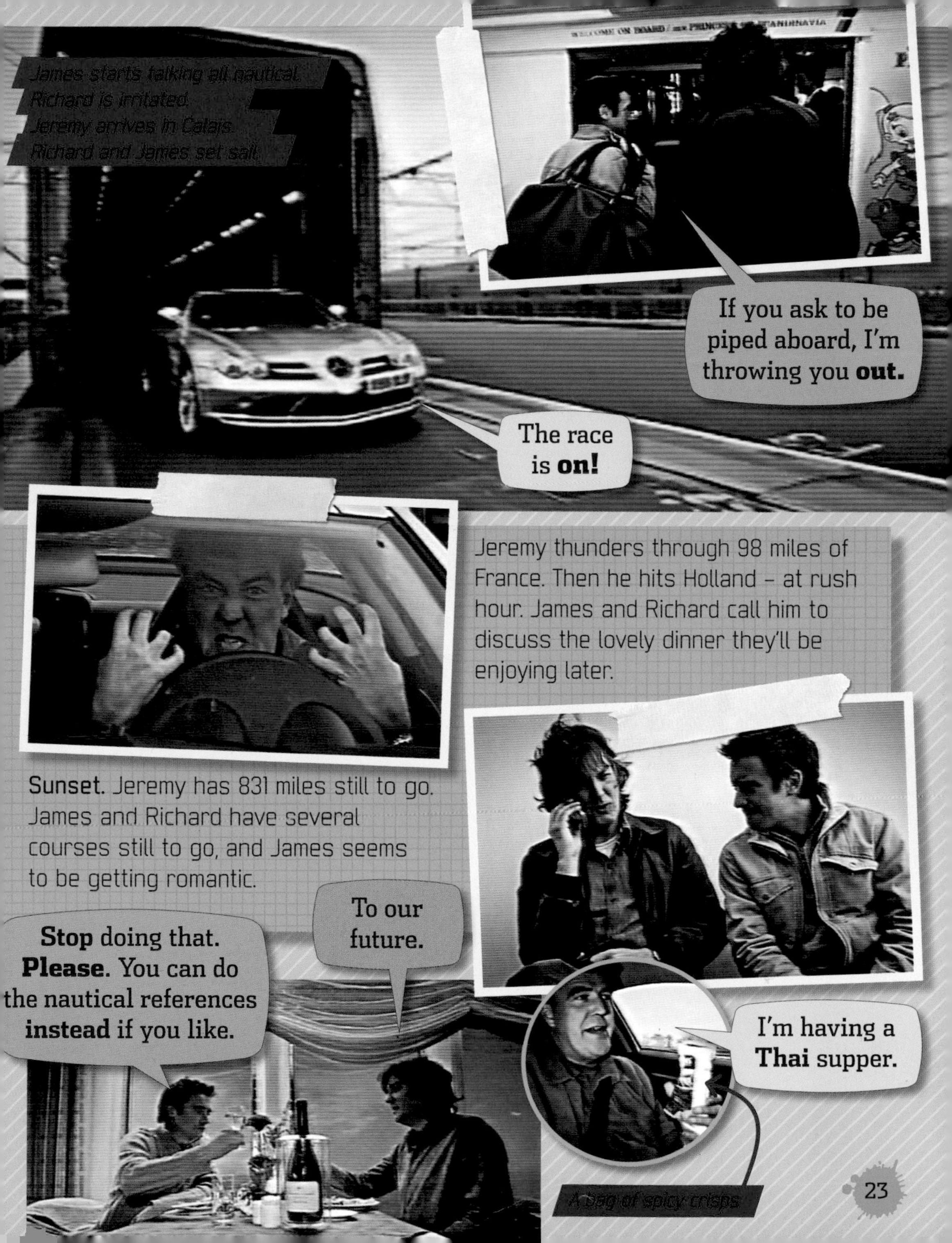
James starts talking all nautical.
Richard is irritated.
Jeremy arrives in Calais.
Richard and James set sail.
If you ask to be piped aboard, I'm throwing you **out.**
The race is **on!**
Jeremy thunders through 98 miles of France. Then he hits Holland – at rush hour. James and Richard call him to discuss the lovely dinner they'll be enjoying later.
**Sunset.** Jeremy has 831 miles still to go. James and Richard have several courses still to go, and James seems to be getting romantic.
To our future.
**Stop** doing that. **Please**. You can do the nautical references **instead** if you like.
I'm having a **Thai** supper.
A bag of spicy crisps

Jeremy heads into yet another country. James and Richard head into a restaurant.
Jeremy winds up the speed as he makes the most of 252 miles of speed-limit-free Autobahn. James and Richard take in a stage show, then

Before he knows it, Jeremy's in Denmark. And feeling weary. To stay awake he tries energy drinks, coffee and talking to himself.

He'll **have** to stop.
It's midnight. After 12 hours, Jeremy's halfway. James is half asleep: he and Richard are tucked up in their (separate) cabin bunks, talking about Jeremy.
Jeremy winds down the window for some reviving Danish air. But...
It's no good. I'm going to **have** to pull over and get some **sleep.**
Jeremy pulls in at a service station near Copenhagen for a kip in the world's most expensive hotel room.
Cramped and cold, Jeremy sets off again at dawn – but he's lost the lead.
As Richard and James have a leisurely breakfast, Jeremy crosses the amazing Oresund Bridge – almost 5 miles long – from Denmark to Sweden.
BRRAAAAARRRR

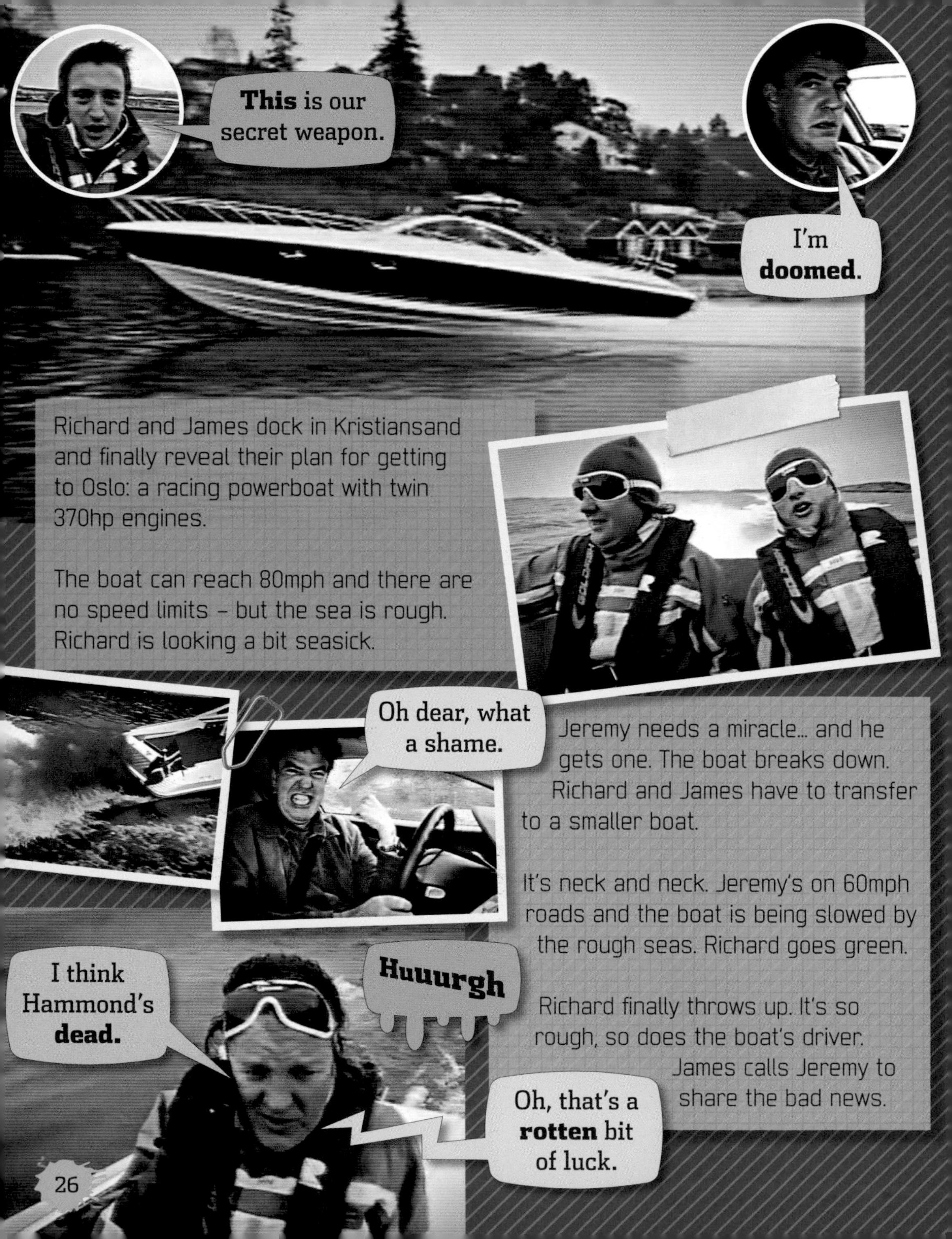


Richard and James dock in Kristiansand and finally reveal their plan for getting to Oslo: a racing powerboat with twin 370hp engines.

The boat can reach 80mph and there are no speed limits – but the sea is rough. Richard is looking a bit seasick.

Jeremy needs a miracle... and he gets one. The boat breaks down. Richard and James have to transfer to a smaller boat.

It's neck and neck. Jeremy's on 60mph roads and the boat is being slowed by the rough seas. Richard goes green.

Richard finally throws up. It's so rough, so does the boat's driver. James calls Jeremy to share the bad news.

Jeremy's only 50 miles from Oslo. James and Richard need to refuel. Then a chamber on their inflatable boat bursts – and the engine's not too healthy either. They're forced to limp to shore.

James and Richard have no idea where they are and their Norwegian is... nonexistent. Then they have to work out how to use a Norwegian cash machine for a bus fare. If they can find a bus.

Jeremy reaches Oslo. Now he just has to find the finish line – marked by a large sculpture of a hand.

They'll **be** here! **What** hand?!

## The Winner

Jeremy reaches the finish and Richard and James are nowhere to be seen. He calls them up to discover they're still lost, somewhere in Norway...

I thought **I'd** had a bad day, but **oh no...**

I made it to Oslo, **flew home** and was halfway through **supper** before these guys arrived at the finishing point.

# Fiat 500 vs BMX bikers

**Can the cute and nippy Fiat 500 (with the less-than-nippy James May at the wheel) win a race across Budapest in Hungary against a couple of BMX stunt bike riders? They'll start in the old part of the city – Buda – and race across the River Danube to an old bicycle factory on the edge of Pest – 8 miles in all.**

## The Competitors

### Fiat 500

This is a retro car built to resemble the original Fiat 500 of the 1950s. It's a lot more sophisticated and comfortable than the original – which was a bit like a rollerskate with a motor – but is it as nimble? Sadly, James will be driving the 1.3-litre, 73bhp turbodiesel, "which is rubbish", he says. This version has a top speed of 102mph and goes from 0-60mph in 12.5 seconds.

### BMX riders

Sebastian Keep and Ben Shenker are professional BMX riders with no fear of death. That's why there are two of them – we hope at least one will make it to the finish.

To borrow the phrase of the **ancient** philosopher Clarksonius... 'How **hard** can it **be?**'

## And They're Off!

James takes an early lead – probably because his vehicle has an engine.

James winds down hairpin bends towards the river. The BMXers take the steps.

James has to stamp on the brakes as the BMXers shoot across the road in front of him.

Despite the shortcuts, the BMXers are struggling to keep up. Mind you, they do keep falling off after overambitious jumps.

But at the snarled-up bridge, James loses his lead.

He overtakes on the other side...

...then gets overtaken again as he hits traffic lights. Which the bikers ignore. Bad lads!

James loses sight of the two-wheeled demons, who have taken an underground shortcut.
SCREEEECH!
CLANGG

CSEPEL MÜVEK
He spots them as they enter the old communist-era industrial estate where the disused bike factory is.
The lead chops and changes – James tries to box in the BMXers behind him, but they just jump over any obstacles.
The final leg through a warehouse: amazingly, James isn't lost, even though the Fiat's satnav is talking to him in Italian.
What?
The finish line's ahead.
Crikey!
I can **see** the flag... I can see **them!**
You **lost!**
Congratulations. Now go and get a **proper** bike.
The Winners
The BMXers win! James swears in Hungarian (well, he claims it's Hungarian).

# Snowmobil vs Icelandic ... on Water

In Iceland, they've created a strange kind of racing. It involves driving ultra-powerful home-made 4x4s up almost vertical cliffs. Well, it helps pass the time in a country where daylight lasts 24 hours in summer. Thing is, these cars are so powerful and have so much grip, they could theoretically drive over water without sinking. So Richard Hammond decided to test that theory.

BA-DOOM

## The Competitors

### Icelandic 4x4

Weld together loads of metal tubes, add a lorry axle and a big Chevrolet V8 engine. Then add nitrous oxide injection to boost the power to over 800bhp, and special wide tyres that will grip just about any surface, and you create one of these. It's very strong. It has to be, as it usually ends up flipping and falling on its roof from a great height.

### Lake Kleifarvatn

It's a lake, made entirely of water. It's 300ft deep, and icy cold. The 'track' is from one side of a bay to the other, a third of mile in all.

### Polaris Snowmobile

This unmodified machine is designed to travel on snow, which is, um, solid. Can it be driven fast enough to skip over the surface of a very liquid lake?

## Race 1: 4x4 vs Lake

Before taking on the snowmobile, Richard had to find out whether the 4x4 will sink or swim. The driver, Icelandic 4x4 racing champion Gísli Gunnar Jónsson, thought it would make it, so Richard strapped himself into the passenger seat. Trusting bloke.



The finish line is 0.5km away on the other side of the lake. Gísli must keep his foot down hard on the accelerator the whole way otherwise he'll lose his jeep.

## And They're Off!

Gísli accelerates hard on the beach. He hits the water. The 4x4 thumps along the surface – if Gísli and Richard were milkshakes, they'd be well frothed. But they don't sink! The theory is right! Gísli hits the other shore.

RRRAAAARRRR

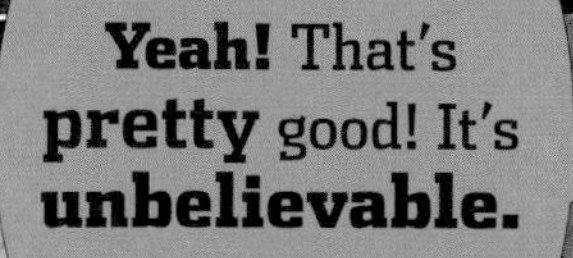

It's a win for insanity and the 4x4.

## Race 2: 4x4 vs Snowmobile

Proving you can do something amazing is one thing. Proving you can beat someone else doing the same amazing thing is even better. So it's Gísli in the 4x4 against another Icelandic chap on a snowmobile: who's fastest on the same stretch of water?

Richard once again rides shotgun in the 4x4 – even he's not mad enough to ride pillion on the snowmobile.

**The Snowmobile:**
A standard Polaris 900 Fusion. 238kg, 292cm long, 2 cylinders, 900cc. And absolutely no floats or inflatable parts.

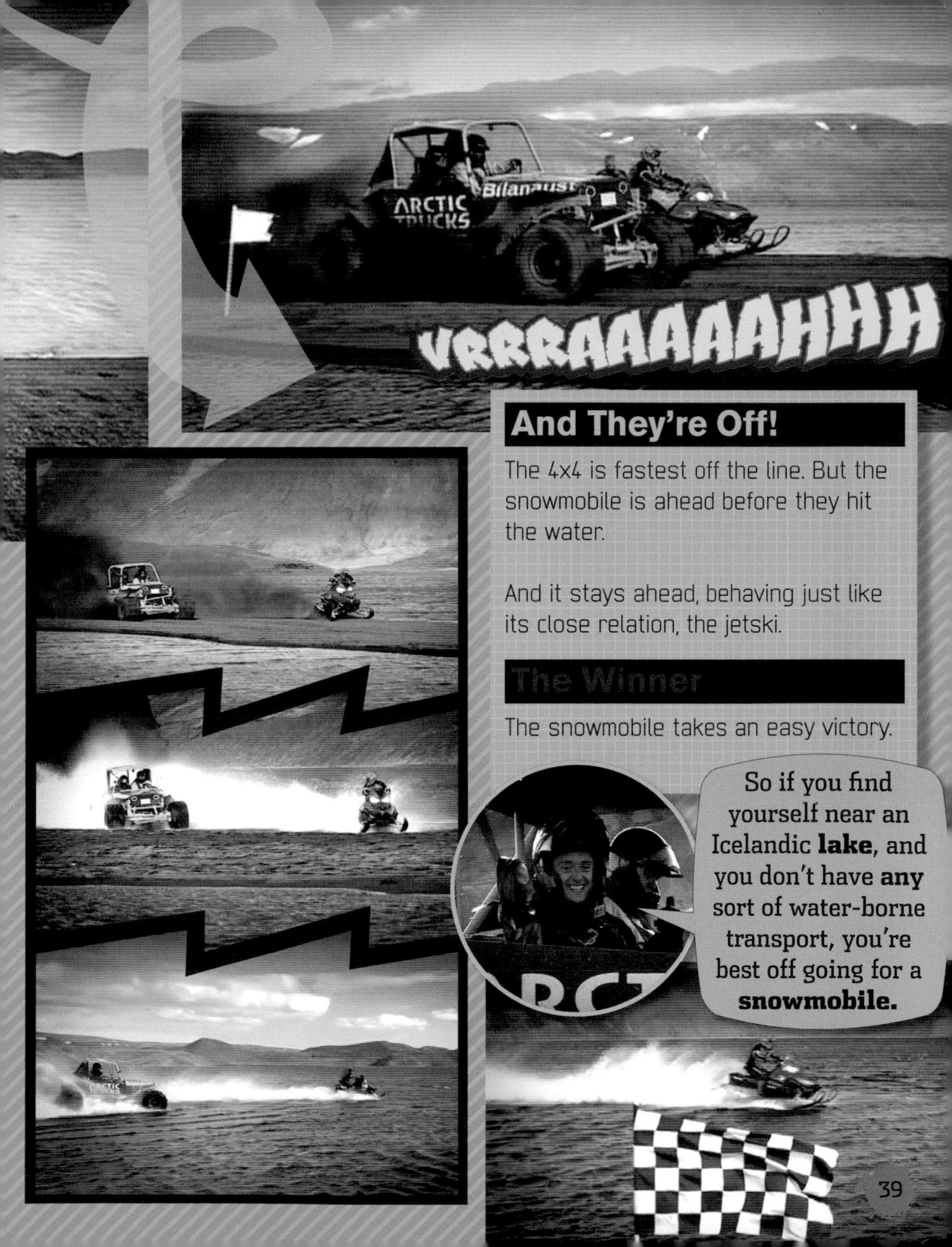


## And They're Off!

The 4x4 is fastest off the line. But the snowmobile is ahead before they hit the water.

And it stays ahead, behaving just like its close relation, the jetski.

## The Winner

The snowmobile takes an easy victory.

# Alf[illegible] Rom[illegible]o 1[illegible] vs Tall Man

**Is a car faster than a man, um, on foot? Surely even Captain Slow himself can't lose this race.**

There's a small problem, though: between the start line and the finish, 1.8 miles away, stands the mile-wide Humber estuary. One-fifth of the rain that lands on England flows out to sea down this stretch of water, which separates Yorkshire from Lincolnshire.

But the Humber is also very shallow. Ermine Street, the old Roman road from London to York, stops on the south bank and continues north – some people think the Romans just waded across. These days there's a bridge, but neither James nor the walker, Graham Boanas, is allowed to use it. James will drive the long way round, via the end of the estuary. Graham will be wading straight across it.

## The Competitors

### The Man

Graham Boanas is 6ft 9in tall (almost 2.06 metres). When you're trying to walk across a river bed, tallness comes in very handy. He has no breathing gear or floats, just a survival suit to keep him dry. He's done this crossing before, but he'll have to do it in 90 minutes to beat James. He might have to try jogging instead of just walking.

### The Car

The Alfa Romeo 159 is a very decent sports saloon from Italy. It's got nice looks, a beautiful 185bhp 2.2-litre engine that will do 0-60mph in 8.5 seconds, and all kinds of electronic gizmos. Sadly it doesn't float, or this race would be over very fast, but on the B-roads and motorways that will form James' 65-mile detour, it handles very nicely.

## And They're Off!

Graham pushes his way through the reeds on the edge of the estuary. Then it's onto his hands and knees to spread his weight and stop him sinking into the thick mud at the water's edge at low tide.

James is bogged down himself, picking his way through quiet villages.

Graham finally gets to his feet and is striding through waist-high water.

The water's shoulder-high on Graham now – he's looking tired as he fights the current trying to wash him away.

James gets onto a stretch of motorway and can really put his foot down.

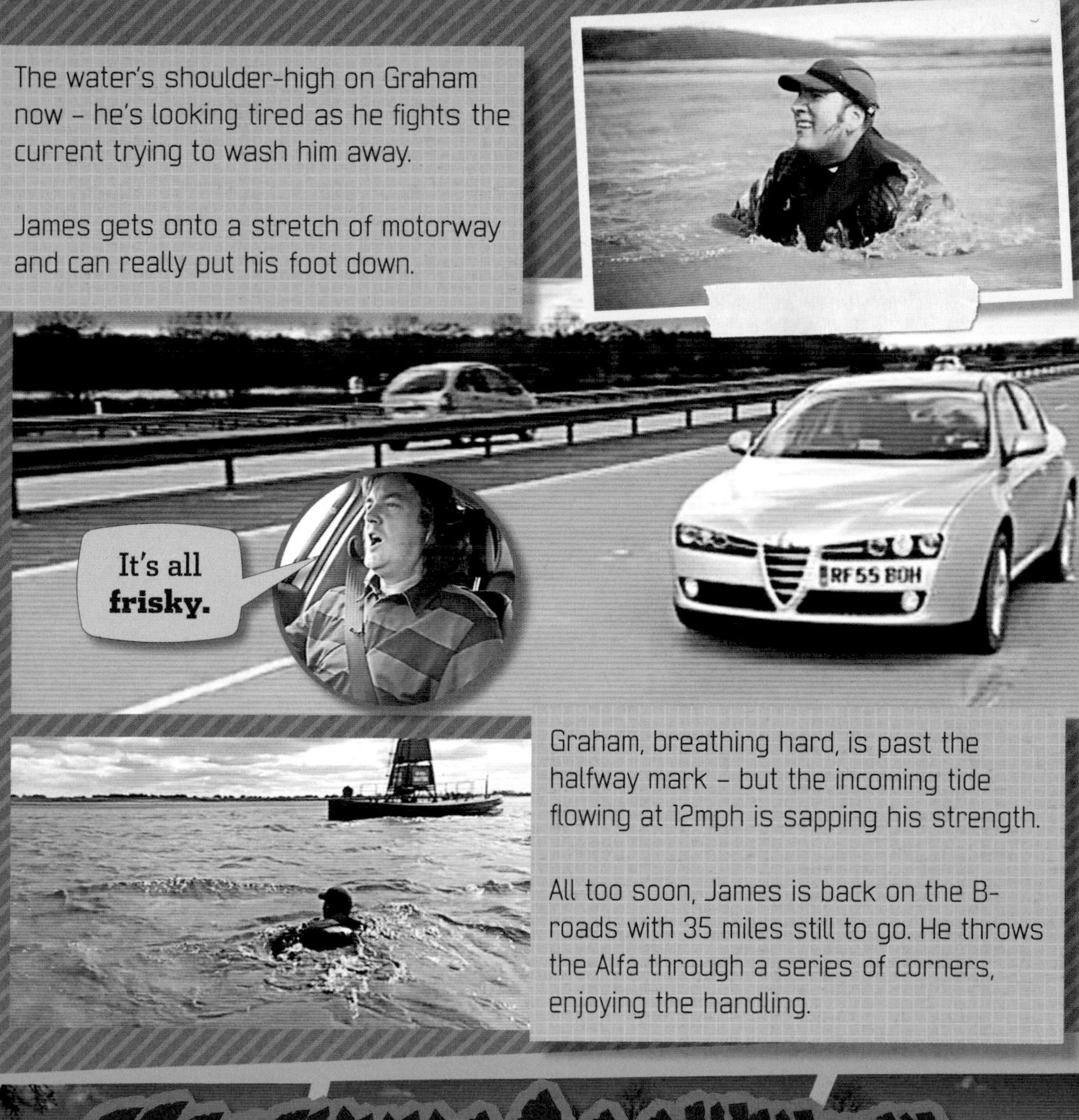


Graham, breathing hard, is past the halfway mark – but the incoming tide flowing at 12mph is sapping his strength.

All too soon, James is back on the B-roads with 35 miles still to go. He throws the Alfa through a series of corners, enjoying the handling.

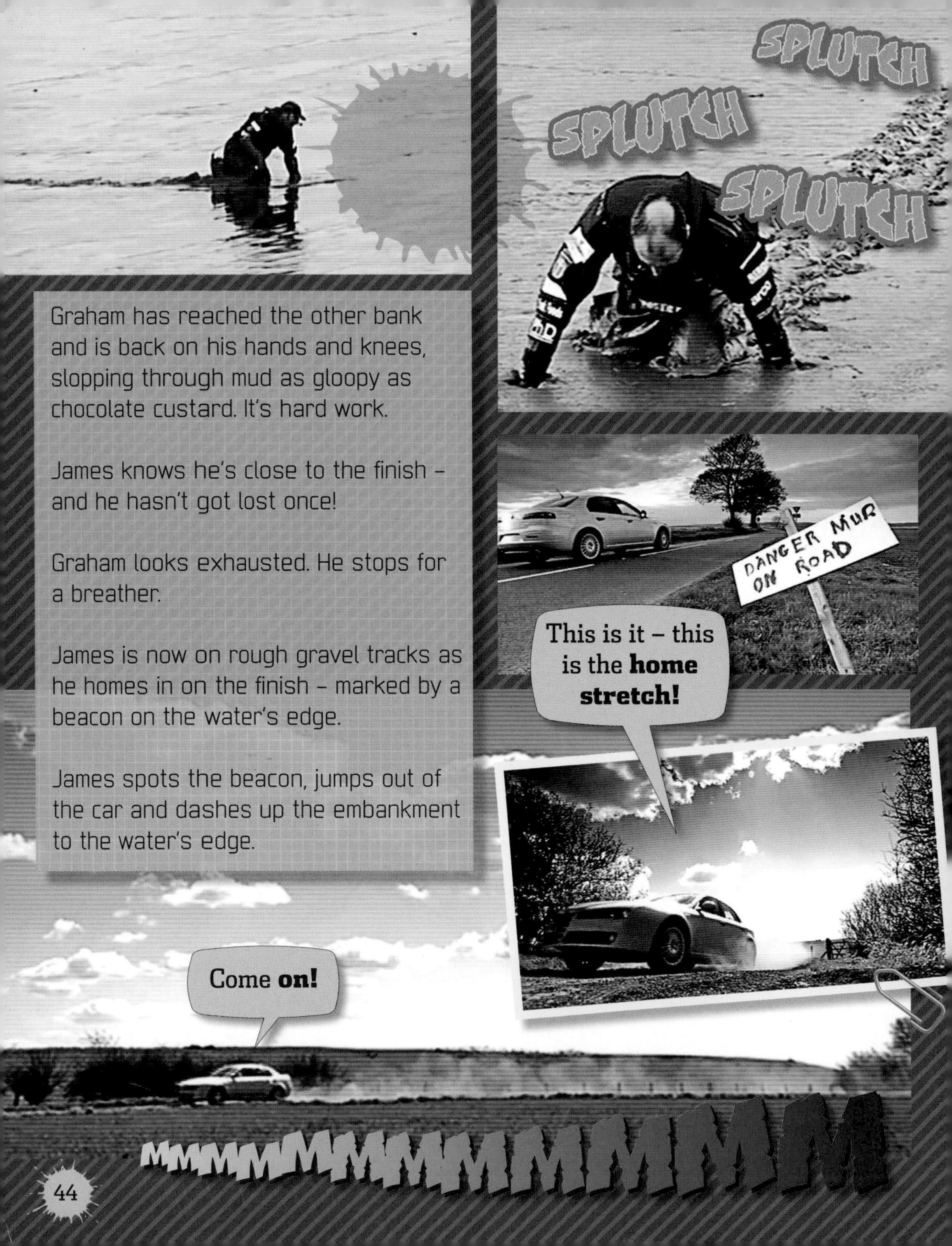


Graham has reached the other bank and is back on his hands and knees, slopping through mud as gloopy as chocolate custard. It's hard work.

James knows he's close to the finish – and he hasn't got lost once!

Graham looks exhausted. He stops for a breather.

James is now on rough gravel tracks as he homes in on the finish – marked by a beacon on the water's edge.

James spots the beacon, jumps out of the car and dashes up the embankment to the water's edge.

## The Winner

But Graham is already there, mud-spattered but back on his feet. James has lost yet another race! Graham offers his muddy hand to shake.

# Glossary

## GPS

A gadget that can tell you your exact position on the planet to within a couple of metres – so obviously James May doesn't own one. A GPS reads a signal beamed down from a series of satellites orbiting the earth. The letters stands for 'Global Positioning System'.

## Hairpin

A 180-degree bend on a mountain road – one so tight you have to slow right down and turn the wheel as far as it will go. Such bends are the same shape as one of the clips women use to keep long hair in place. Assuming you know what one of those clips looks like. And you probably don't. Why would you? So here's a picture of a hairpin bend instead.

## Harridan

A vicious, scolding woman. You might have met one or two of these at school.

## Nitrous oxide

Most cars are powered by 'internal combustion' engines. These produce power by sucking a mixture of fuel (usually petrol) and air (which contains oxygen) into the cylinders and igniting it with a bang – that's why engines are so noisy. If you inject nitrous oxide gas into

the cylinders too, it produces more oxygen, which makes a bigger bang, which makes more power. Unless the engine isn't built strongly enough, in which case the bigger bang just blows it apart instead. Use nitrous oxide injection with care, and never on pets.

## Pillion

The seat behind the rider on a jetski, motorbike, snowmobile, horse, yak etc. Can also mean the person (or other animal) occupying that seat.

## Retro

Old-fashioned-looking, even though it may not be old-fashioned. For instance, James May's hairstyle looks a bit retro, even though it was all grown in the last few months.

## Ride Shotgun

To travel in the passenger seat, alongside the driver. This is the second-best seat in the car after the driver's, because it gives you to control over in-car entertainment and the heating. However, this position makes you vulnerable to attacks from behind by ear-flicking, seat-kicking friends and siblings. Do not carry an actual shotgun on your journey, as this might make the driver nervous.

## Satnav

A computerised map that uses GPS to identify your location and provide directions to your destination. Well, that's the idea. Sometimes the directions are just stupid. You can choose from a range of voices for your satnav unit, but all of them will be really annoying after a while.

## Survival Suit

Also called an Immersion Suit, this is a special, completely waterproof outfit that keeps the wearer dry and warm even when he's floating in the sea. You probably don't have one hanging in your wardrobe, unless you own a fishing trawler.

## Wingsuit

A special one-piece suit with material between the arms and legs, which allows skydivers to glide instead of just dropping straight down. They still need to wear parachutes, though, as a wingsuit won't slow their descent enough to let them land safely. The design of wingsuits was inspired by sugar gliders and flying squirrels, animals that have skin webs which allow them to glide from tree to tree.

## Thames Barrier

The series of huge river gates east of London that protect the city, preventing it from flooding after unusually high tides. The Thames Barrier was completed in 1984 and it has been raised more than 100 times since. Sea levels are rising around the world due to global warming, so every year it has to be used more often. If it fails, then London will probably become known as "The Venice of the North" and the Congestion Charge will apply to boats, too.